BIBLE 120
WISDOM

MW01121115

CONTENTS

Author: **Barry G. Burrus, M.Div, M.A., B.S.**

Editor: Alan Christopherson, M.S.

Illustrations: Stephen J. Missal

                    Kyle R. Bennett, A.S.

                    Alpha Omega Graphics

Alpha Omega Publications ®

300 North McKemy Avenue, Chandler, Arizona 85226-2618
© MM by Alpha Omega Publications, Inc.   All rights reserved.
LIFEPAC is a registered trademark of Alpha Omega Publications, Inc.

BIBLE 1209
WISDOM

CONTENTS

I. DAVID AND SOLOMON

II. GOD'S ATTRIBUTES

III. THE HEBREW NATURE

WISDOM

David and Solomon's lives, which are recorded in the Old Testament, are profitable examples for modern living. Their writings portray wisdom that transcends boundaries of culture and time.

David's pain and victory, as expressed in the Psalms, are timeless. He submitted to God his honest complaints and enthusiastic thanks. In turn, God honored him. Constant communication was the essence of his and God's relationship.

Solomon, David's tenth son, became king upon his father's death. Solomon knew that he was young and inexperienced and needed the LORD's guidance in ruling Israel. He prayed that God would give him an understanding heart to judge the people. God was pleased with him and granted his requests, adding unto him riches and honor. His prayer for wisdom was vital to his relationship to God.

Difficult decisions were made on the basis of God's wisdom rather than fallen human intellect.

The wisdom Solomon used to rule Israel was recorded primarily in the form of proverbs. Proverbs are short rules of conduct that give practical moral guidance. They are succinct answers to everyday dilemmas that are useful when giving counsel.

The various styles of the Biblical writers add extra interest to God's message. By God's design, reading His Word is enjoyable and challenging. In this LIFEPAC® you will study the practical application of Psalms and Proverbs. You will analyze the Bible's various literary forms and study how it clarifies problems, guides you in expressing joy and solving difficulties.

OBJECTIVES

Read these objectives. The objectives tell you what you will be able to do when you have successfully completed this LIFEPAC.

When you have completed this LIFEPAC, you should be able to:

1. Identify significant events in the lives of David and Solomon.

2. List David's character qualities.

3. Identify instances when the LORD specifically guided David and Solomon.

4. Identify prominent people and places in their lives.

5. Identify the cause of Solomon's downfall.

6. Identify Scriptural examples of sanctification, comfort, God's omnipresence, His sovereignty, and guidance.

7. Describe the importance of wisdom in problem solving.

8. Name three types of Davidic Psalms.

9. Describe Biblical literary styles.

10. Identify New Testament fulfillment of Old Testament prefiguration.

Survey the LIFEPAC. Ask yourself some questions about this study. Write your questions here.

_____

_____

_____

_____

_____

_____

_____

_____

_____

I. DAVID AND SOLOMON

In Scripture, people are authentic, and their personalities are not hidden from the reader. They show God leading His people.

You can learn much by comparing yourself and your goals with those of certain biblical characters. David's life is a good example. Young David had to establish himself as an adult. He was responsible to protect and care for sheep, which prepared him to care for a nation. As David grew into a man, he recognized the need to evaluate his own strengths and weaknesses. His society was a challenging environment in which to become an adult, but he readily accepted the challenge.

The mature David was a warrior-king and a merciful leader. Step by step, and battle by battle, God established him as king in Jerusalem.

SECTION OBJECTIVES

Review these objectives. When you have completed this section, you should be able to:

1. Identify significant events in the lives of David and Solomon.
2. List David's character qualities.
3. Identify instances when the LORD specifically guided David and Solomon.
4. Identify prominent people and places in their lives.

VOCABULARY

Study these words to enhance your learning success in this section.

apostasy	ephah	pestilence	remorse	threshingfloor
covenant	expertise	prudent	supplication	

Note: All vocabulary words in this LIFEPAC appear in **boldface** print the first time they are used. If you are unsure of the meaning when you are reading, study the definitions given.

 Read 1 Samuel chapters 16-25 and 2 Samuel chapters 11-13.

DAVID'S LIFE

God endowed David with many kingly qualities including strength, perceptiveness, and hospitality. David was chosen to replace Saul as Israel's king after Saul disobeyed the LORD and thus, lost his throne. Although David was a king, he was not immune to temptation or sin. Unlike most, he acknowledged his sin and was strengthened by God in his office, private life, and friendships.

Anointed king. God commanded Saul to kill the Amalekites and "...utterly destroy all that they have, and spare them not; but slay both man and woman, infant and suckling, ox and sheep, camel and ass" (1 Samuel 15:3). Instead, Saul's troops spared the best of the sheep and oxen for sacrifices. He did not kill Agag (the Amalekite king), but brought him back as a prisoner. Samuel declared to Saul " ...Because thou hast rejected the word of the LORD, he hath also rejected thee from *being* king" (1 Samuel 15:23). Samuel himself then killed Agag to fulfill God's command to Saul.

God sent Samuel to Bethlehem to anoint a new king from Jesse's sons. Samuel feared that Saul would murder him if he found out his intentions. Therefore, God told Samuel to take a heifer with him as a sacrifice in order to give him a public reason for going. Seven of Jesse's sons passed before Samuel, but none of them were the chosen king. When David (Jesse's youngest son) was brought in, Samuel anointed him and the LORD'S Spirit came upon him.

Goliath. The Israeli and Philistine war camps had been arrayed in battle for forty days. Jesse sent David to deliver bread and an **ephah** of parched corn to feed his brothers, who were part of the army. When David arrived at the battlefield, he could not understand the Israelites' fear of the Philistines. He

SAMUEL DISGUISED HIS PURPOSE IN GOING TO BETHLEHEM.

that his faith was in the power of God and not in his own resources.

Alone with his sheep for long periods of time, David disciplined his body and spirit, increasing his physical and spiritual strength. In the privacy of the fields, David talked to God. He grew in spiritual knowledge and understanding.

David expressed himself through his psalms. The Psalms include hymns, **supplications**, and thanksgivings he accompanied with his harp. A crowned leader is no different in God's eyes than the humblest Christian who speaks to the LORD from their heart.

knew no one could successfully defy God's armies. He challenged the soldiers for their lack of courage against Goliath, the Philistine armored giant who was insulting God's people.

David's oldest brother Eliab, mistook David's faith as pride and became very angry. Eliab thought David belonged back in the wilderness with his sheep, and accused him of coming just to watch the battle.

David was **prudent** in speech, choosing his words carefully. When taken to Saul for permission to fight Goliath, he convincingly spoke of his courage and ability to stand against the giant.

In the fields, David protected his sheep by killing lions and bears. His experience proved God had already prepared him to fight the giant. David said, "...the LORD that delivered me out of the paw of the lion, and out of the paw of the bear, he will deliver me out of the hand of this Philistine" (1 Samuel 17:37). David clearly stated

DAVID DISCIPLINED HIS BODY AND SOUL.

Answer these questions.

1.1   How did Saul disobey God? _____

_____

_____

1.2   Why did Samuel disguise his purpose for going to the house of Jesse?

_____

1.3   What is an ephah? _____

1.4   What kinds of Psalms did David write?

     a. _____

     b. _____

     c. _____

Jonathan. Saul's eldest son, Jonathan, immediately loved David as his own soul. He gave David his own armor and clothing, symbolizing the giving over of his own royalty, "...even to his sword, and to his bow, and to his girdle" (1 Samuel 18:4). Jonathan was loyal to David, not Saul, as king.

Saul grew furiously jealous of David and tried to assassinate him, but Jonathan convinced Saul that David was innocent of any wrongdoing against his throne or person, for he served his father well. For a time Saul was appeased, but Jonathan eventually realized the seriousness of his father's actions and helped David to flee.

Through narrow escapes, Jonathan warned David of Saul's wrath and helped Him to escape into the fields. Michal, Saul's daughter and David's first wife, helped David escape through a window.

David and Jonathan established a **covenant** relationship. They vowed, "...The LORD be between me and thee, and between my seed and thy seed for ever..." (1 Samuel 20:42).

In spite of Saul's treachery, David spared his life twice. In a cave at Engedi, David inched close enough to Saul to cut off a piece of the royal robe without the king detecting his presence. At Ziph, David snatched a spear and jug of water from Saul's side. The king remained asleep, and in the morning had to send someone over to David's camp to reclaim the weapon.

After Jonathan and Saul's deaths, David wrote a lament, a poetical expression of grief and sorrow: "The beauty of Israel is slain upon thy high places:

JONATHAN WARNED DAVID OF SAUL'S WRATH.

how are the mighty fallen!" (2 Samuel 1:19) Once king, David sought out Jonathan's lame son, Mephibosheth, in order to honor him. Mephibosheth was frightened in the presence of the king, saying "...What *is* thy servant, that thou shouldest look upon such a dead dog as I *am*?" (2 Samuel 9:8) David reassured him and brought Mephibosheth's household to live in Jerusalem where they ate continually at the king's table.

Complete these sentences.

1.5 Jonathan gave David his own a. _____ and b. _____ as a symbol of his dedication and love for David.

1.6 Jonathan realized the seriousness of Saul's threats and helped David to _____ .

1.7 On two occasions David spared _____ life.

1.8 In a cave at _____ , David cut off a piece of Saul's robe.

1.9 David snatched a a. _____ and b. _____ from Saul's bolster.

1.10 David and Jonathan had a _____ relationship.

Answer this question.

1.11 What is a lament? _____

Adultery, Murder, and the Census. The LORD'S greatest displeasure with David came when he allowed Bathsheba's beauty to lure him into sin. Several tragic consequences resulted from their adultery. Bathsheba became pregnant and the unrepentant David chose to cover his sin by arranging the murder of her husband, Uriah. Even the most faithful Christian could suddenly find themselves trapped in a web of their own sin.

Uriah's murder did not put an end to David's problems. He also had to suffer the loss of their child. Sin almost always affects other people. David's sin affected not only himself but also Bathsheba, Uriah, and an innocent baby. The LORD was angered over the effect David's sin would have on those who already mocked God (2 Samuel 12:14). The LORD jealously guards the holiness of His name.

David's deep **remorse** upon realizing the effects of sin upon himself, others, and the God he loved is expressed in Psalm 51. With candid honesty, he outpoured his desire to be purified and renewed. He longed to be back in fellowship with the God of his salvation.

Even though David petitioned with prayer and fasting, the child died. David married Bathsheba; and God later blessed her with the birth of Solomon, Israel's future king.

Absalom was another of David's sons. He was exiled for murdering of his half-brother, Amnon. Because David's love for his son was so great, the years Absalom spent in exile were torturous. Soon after his return, Absalom began to divide the kingdom, openly criticizing and undermining his father's authority. In the end, even though Absalom's army set forth against David's, the tortured father still requested that the soldiers be gentle with his son.

As Absalom was riding his mule away from the battlegrounds one day, his hair became caught in the branches of an oak tree and the mule went out from under him. Joab thrust three spears into Absalom's heart as he dangled helplessly from the tree. David mourned openly and bitterly for his beloved Absalom.

David also sinned in ordering a census in Israel. As a result, the LORD sent a **pestilence** upon the land. David prayed that God would be merciful to the people and punish him alone. After the prayer, the prophet Gad came to him with instructions from the LORD to build an altar in Araunah's **threshingfloor**.

Araunah, a working man in David's kingdom, probably derived his living from his threshingfloor and oxen. Surprised by the king's visit, Araunah learned that David sought to buy his threshingfloor to build an altar. Araunah, behaving in a kingly manner himself, offered to give David the floor and the oxen so that the king could give offerings to God. Araunah, who was willing to part with his material possessions, honored David's position as king and respected God's freedom to deal in His own way with David. David purchased the threshingfloor from Araunah and built an altar. God ended the pestilence upon Israel.

Conqueror. David's enemies included more than pagan invaders. Incited by an unfounded jealousy, Saul himself became David's enemy. In his aging years, David had to defend his own throne from the young usurpers who anticipated his death.

From the time that David killed Goliath, he left the fields of sheep and exchanged them for fields of battle: "And David went out whithersoever Saul sent him, *and* behaved himself wisely: and Saul set him over the men of war, and he was accepted in the sight of all the people, and also in the sight of Saul's servants" (1 Samuel 18:5). In fact, David was so well received that the people began to chant a praise, "…Saul hath slain his thousands, and David his ten thousands" (1 Samuel 18:7).

When the Philistines had overpowered Keilah, the LORD directed David to attack. Although David saved Keilah and smote the Philistines, Saul was still intent on destroying him. Saul was not dissuaded by David's victories on his behalf, he continued to track the one he thought threatened his throne.

After Saul's death, David went into Judah where he was anointed king, but Saul's influences were still strong. He was not anointed king of Israel until he had reigned for almost eight years in Judah. According to 2 Samuel 3:1, "…there was long war between the house of Saul and the house of David: but David waxed stronger and stronger, and the house of Saul waxed weaker and weaker."

Answer these questions.

1.12 Who were the three people whose deaths caused David much grief?

a. _____

b. _____

c. _____

1.13 What were two direct consequences of the sin between David and Bathsheba?

_____

_____

1.14 In what Psalm does David express his deep remorse for his sin? _____

1.15 Why was Absalom sent into exile? _____

_____

1.16 Why did David regret taking a census? _____

_____

Match these items.

1.17 _____ Jonathan's lame son   a. Bathsheba

1.18 _____ killed Absalom   b. David

1.19 _____ Bathsheba's first husband   c. Uriah

1.20 _____ David's first wife   d. Araunah

1.21 _____ Solomon's mother   e. Michal

1.22 _____ Jonathan's father   f. Mephibosheth

1.23 _____ writer of Psalm 51   g. Joab

1.24 _____ sold a threshingfloor to David   h. Saul

Answer *true* or *false*.

1.25 _____ Saul and David always had a peaceful relationship.

1.26 _____ David had to defend his own throne.

1.27 _____ David was not accepted by the people of Saul's kingdom.

1.28 _____ David attacked Keilah in defense of the Philistines.

1.29 _____ When Saul died, David was anointed king of Judah.

 Read 1 Samuel 16:18 and 2 Samuel chapter 22.

CHARACTER

Each individual has unique personality characteristics that influence their interactions. David was eager for God's guidance.

God anointed David and developed his kingly qualities. These qualities spurred him into battle, gained victories, and caused him to mature.

Bravery. David grew up learning the importance of bravery. The very nature of his occupation demanded it. He took seriously his responsibility of protecting his herd of sheep from danger. He knew that cowardliness in the face of shadows and sounds of the night could cost him his life and the lives of his sheep.

David lived courageously, for God gave him reason to be unafraid. As seen in his bold confrontation with Goliath, David knew God was on his side and that the result would be Goliath's death.

Another example was David's night visit to Saul's camp. While Saul and his entire army slept, David slipped Saul's spear and water jug from where the king was sleeping and left the camp. David risked his own life to prove to Saul that he did not desire to kill him.

Mercy. On several occasions, David had excellent opportunities to kill Saul. The fact that David spared Saul's life is an example of mercy.

Second Samuel 19 records a similar account. Shimei, a Benjamite son of Gera, was guilty of hurling insults at King David. When Shimei fell before the king and begged his forgiveness, David's response was, "...Thou shalt not die..." (2 Samuel 19:23).

Humility. David's Psalms reflect his humility. He was keenly aware of his servanthood to God and knew he was totally dependent upon Him.

Following David's victory over Hadadezar, Toi's son Joram brought vessels of silver, gold, and brass to the king (2 Samuel 8:10-11). Toi siezed the vessels as a result of his own previous victory over Hadadezar. He sent the gifts to David to salute and bless him for his victory. Instead of proud acceptance of Toi's praise, David "...did dedicate unto the LORD, with the silver and gold that he had dedicated of all nations which he subdued" (2 Samuel 8:11). David was acting in humble admission that the victories were a result of God's power and might and not his own.

Shrewdness. David was a keen businessman. He organized and executed his administration so that Israel prospered. He was wise in matters of commerce, agriculture, justice, and God's law.

David had great military **expertise** which could be measured in his many successes on the battlefield. In Hebron, respected representatives of each tribe claimed Him king and anointed ruler over all of Israel. He won back Jerusalem and established it as the city of David. Battle after

BRAVERY: A QUALITY OF *DAVID'S* CHARACTER

battle, he outflanked the Philistines in the valley of Rephaim and crushed their force from Geba to Gazer (2 Samuel 5:25).

After the Ark of the Covenant was joyously housed in Jerusalem, David continued to conquer. He smote Methgammah, Moab, and Zobah where he moved to reestablish his border at the Euphrates River. Even when many Syrians and Ammonites united, forming twenty thousand soldiers to encircle the troops of Joab, David and Joab continued to conquer. The LORD gave David his victories.

In time, David's battles decreased in number and intensity. The few strategic conflicts at the end of his life were largely associated with fending off those attempting to usurp his throne.

Prayerfulness. David's life was dependent upon God. He was aware of his own sinfulness and continually sought the LORD'S guidance in his leadership.

Being an Old Testament saint, David was careful to know God's specific will, especially in military matters. For example, in 1 Samuel 23:1-4, David prayed to the LORD for guidance in defending Keilah against the Philistines. David obeyed, never questioning God.

 Complete these sentences.

1.30   David's choosing to spare Saul's life is an example of his _____ .

1.31   David's prayers were followed by _____ .

7

Complete this activity.

1.32   Read 2 Samuel 22, and write a two-page paper about David's character as reflected in the passage.

 Score _____

Adult check _____

                Initial   Date

 Read 1 Kings chapters 1, 2, 5, and 11.

SOLOMON'S LIFE

Absalom's half brother Adonijah sought to seize Israel's throne while his father David was in need of constant care (Abishag, a Shunamite woman, was brought in to minister to David) and was dying of old age. David was unaware that Adonijah had readied chariots and horsemen or had solicited the support of Abiathar (the priest) and Joab (commander of David's troops). They made preparations for a feast to honor him as the new king.

Nathan (the prophet) discussed Adonijah's actions with Bathsheba and advised her to speak with David and influence him to officially announce that Solomon would be his successor. While Bathsheba was talking with David in his chamber, Nathan came in to confirm and support her story. David assured them that Solomon would be the new king. David requested that Nathan and Zadok (the priest) take Solomon to the spring of Gihon and anoint him king over Israel. David's sudden action terrified Adonijah, and he went to the Temple and pleaded for Solomon to spare his life.

Before his death, David gave guidelines to Solomon and identified those whom he should wisely attack and those he should show kindness. If Solomon would obey the LORD'S laws, He would keep the covenant that David's descendants would remain on the throne forever.

Significantly related to Israel's peace was Solomon's request for wisdom. When the LORD appeared to Solomon in a dream, Solomon said, "Give therefore thy servant an understanding heart to judge thy people, that I may discern between good and bad: for who is able to judge this thy so great a people?" (1 Kings 3:9) Flourishing under Solomon's leadership, God made Israel one of the most materially and spiritually rich kingdoms of the ancient world.

Solomon raised a labor levy to build the Temple and palace. From conquered towns, Solomon used the Amorites, Hittites, Perizzites, Hivites, and Jubusites. The work was regulated by Israelite soldiers, princes, captains, and rulers. Solomon initiated a navy and secured a naval fleet to sail the Red Sea.

After the Temple and the palace of Solomon were completed, the LORD appeared to Solomon a second time. He assured Solomon that He had heard his prayers and blessed the Temple. In the vision, He reminded Solomon to walk before Him with integrity of heart and obedience. God warned Solomon of the consequences of serving false gods: "*But* if ye shall at all turn from following me … Then will I cut off Israel out of the land which I have given them; and this house, which I have hallowed for my name, will I cast out of my sight…" (1 Kings 9:67).

Solomon married the Pharaoh's daughter as well as Moabite, Ammonite, Edomite, Zidonian, and Hittite women. God had repeatedly instructed and warned not to intermarry with pagans. However, "…Solomon clave unto these [wives] in love" (1 Kings 11:2). As he grew older, they influenced him to build altars on Jerusalem's hills for their gods. Solomon's disobedience brought forth God's rebuke: "…Forasmuch as this is done of thee, and thou hast not kept my covenant and my statutes, which I have commanded thee, I will surely rend the kingdom from thee, and will give it to thy servant. Notwithstanding in thy days I will not do it for David thy father's sake: *but* I will rend it out of the hand of thy son. Howbeit I will not rend away all the kingdom; *but* will give one tribe to thy son for David my servant's sake, and for Jerusalem's sake which I have chosen" (1 Kings 11:11-13). After his **apostasy**, the peace of the kingdom was broken.

8

Complete these statements.

1.33   Absalom's half brother, _____ , wanted to become king of Israel.

1.34   Joab and _____ , the priest, supported Adonijah's efforts to seize the throne.

1.35   Nathan advised _____ to speak with David regarding Adonijah's actions.

1.36   A Shunamite woman named _____ ministered to David in his old age.

1.37   Solomon was anointed king near the spring of _____ .

1.38   Solomon formed a _____ levy to build the Temple and palace.

1.39   Solomon asked God for _____ .

Answer *true* **or** *false.*

1.40   _____ God instructed his chosen people not to intermarry with Israelites.

1.41   _____ Israel's peaceful state came to an end following Solomon's apostasy.

1.42   _____ Solomon's wives influenced him to destroy all pagan altars.

1.43   _____ Solomon secured a naval fleet to sail the Red Sea.

1.44   _____ God did not warn Solomon about the consequences of worshiping false gods.

Read 1 Kings chapter 3; 4:20-34; and chapters 6-7.

RICHES

Victory and obedience describes David's reign; whereas peace, wealth, and wisdom describe Solomon's. Each generation has its own social atmosphere and spiritual mission, developing different qualities to attain its goals. Solomon's riches were both material and spiritual. For posterity, Solomon recorded much of his wisdom in the form of proverbs.

Material. Provisions were brought to Solomon's household every day. Each and every day Solomon's household used "...thirty measures of fine flour, and threescore measures of meal, ten fat oxen, and twenty oxen out of the pastures, and an hundred sheep, besides harts, and roebucks, and fallowdeer, and fatted fowl" (1 Kings 4:22-23). Straw and barley were provided every day for Solomon's forty thousand horses and camels. The kingdom's land area was broad enough to be divided into twelve large sections. Each one had an appointed officer responsible for one month out of each year to obtain and transport the necessities.

Hiram, king of Tyre, rejoiced when he heard that Solomon would build the Temple. He had shared in the Temple plans with David and wanted to assist Solomon by providing the cedar to build much of it. In exchange, Solomon gave Hiram twenty thousand measures of wheat and twenty measures of pure oil each year, which typified their whole relationship. Solomon levied thirty thousand men to work in Lebanon to obtain material.

The Temple itself was extremely elaborate, with deep porches and many interior and exterior chambers. The interior walls and floor were made of cedar and overlaid with pure gold. Within the oracle were two identical cherubims carved from olive trees. "And he set the cherubims within the inner house: and they stretched forth the wings of the cherubims, so that the wing of the one touched the *one* wall, and the wing of the other cherub touched the other wall; and their wings touched one another in the midst of the house. And he overlaid the cherubims with gold" (1 Kings 6:27-28). The talented Hiram (a bronze worker from Tyre) cast bronze columns for the Temple porch. He also made a water source called a molten sea that stood upon twelve oxen. According to 1 Kings 7:26, "... it *was* an handbreadth thick, and the brim thereof was wrought like the brim of a cup, with flowers of lilies: it contained two thousand baths."

After hearing intriguing statements concerning Solomon's wealth and wisdom, the queen of Sheba decided to visit the king. The queen shared with Solomon all that was on her heart and he answered all of her questions. The queen brought gold, spices, and jewels to Solomon, and he gave her all that she desired from his kingdom. She said to Solomon, "...thy wisdom and prosperity exceedeth the fame which I heard" (1 Kings 10:7).

Spiritual. David left a legacy of spirituality to Solomon and advised him to "...keep the charge of the LORD thy God, to walk in his way, to keep his statutes, and his commandments, and his judgments, and his testimonies, as it is written in the law of Moses..." (1 Kings 2:3). From the beginning of his reign as king, Solomon "...loved the LORD, walking in the statutes of David his father..." (1 Kings 3:3).

Solomon had a dream in Gibeon where he had offered a thousand burnt offerings upon the altar. In it, God told Solomon to ask for whatever he desired. Solomon responded, telling the LORD that he felt a heavy responsibility, and admitted that he was but a little child, not knowing how to go out or to come in (1 Kings 3:7). Solomon, asking for discernment, said, "...For who is able to judge this thy so great a people?" (1 Kings 3:9) Pleased by Solomon's humble request, the LORD blessed him with a wise and an understanding heart. In addition, God blessed him with riches and honor.

On one occasion, Solomon's wisdom was demonstrated in settling a conflict between two distraught mothers. First Kings 3:16-28 records the account of two harlots who each gave birth to a son. The women were living together in the same house and the babies were born three days apart. When one of the babies died, his mother placed the child's dead body in the arms of the other mother while she slept. It was Solomon's responsibility to decide who was the real mother of the living child. Solomon determined the rightful mother by calling for a sword and ordering that the child be divided in two. Each mother had a different response: "...O my lord, give her the living child, and in no wise slay it. But the other said, Let it be neither mine nor thine, *but* divide *it*" (1 Kings 3:26). Solomon quickly recognized that the real mother was the one who wanted the child to live.

"And God gave Solomon wisdom and understanding exceeding much, and largeness of heart, even as the sand that *is* on the sea shore... And he spake three thousand proverbs: and his songs were a thousand and five ... And there came of all people to hear the wisdom of Solomon, from all kings of the earth, which had heard of his wisdom" (1 Kings 4:29-34).

Answer these questions.

1.45   What was David's advice to Solomon? _____

_____

1.46   What was the responsibility of each of the twelve sections of Solomon's kingdom?

_____

_____

1.47   What was Solomon's greatest contribution to future generations? _____

_____

1.48   What building materials were used for the interior walls and floors of the Temple?

_____

_____

1.49   How did Solomon discover the identity of the real mother of the living child?

_____

_____

_____

Match these items.

1.50 _____ cherubims   a. where the Ark of the Covenant was joyously housed

1.51 _____ Hiram   b. home of one of Solomon's wives

1.52 _____ Gibeon   c. place where Solomon had a dream

1.53 _____ Sheba   d. provided cedar for the Temple

1.54 _____ Jerusalem   e. sat within the oracle of the Temple

1.55 _____ Egypt   f. a queen who brought gifts to Solomon

Score _____

Adult check _____

                    Initial   **Date**

Review the material in this section in preparation for the Self Test. This Self Test will check your mastery of this particular section. The items missed on this Self Test will indicate specific areas where restudy is needed for mastery.

Choose the correct answer (each answer, 2 points).

1.01   David was _____ in speech.

    a. redundant   b. prudent   c. indiscreet

1.02   The Psalms that David composed were supplications, thanksgivings, and _____ .

    a. hymns   b. orations   c. proverbs

1.03   David's relationship to God was enriched by _____ .

    a. wealth   b. battles   c. prayer

1.04   Samuel took a _____ to Bethlehem for a sacrificial offering.

    a. heifer   b. goat   c. dove

1.05   Solomon exiled the priest, _____ for his aid to Adonijah.

    a. Hiram   b. Abiathar   c. Nathan

1.06   David had a covenant relationship with _____ .

    a. Saul   b. Jonathan   c. Samuel

1.07   David's grief over the deaths of some loved ones caused him to write _____ .

    a. a proverb   b. a lament   c. a eulogy

1.08   In the cave at _____ , David cut off a piece of Saul's robe.

    a. Ziph   b. Edom   c. Engedi

1.09   Saul disobeyed God in not killing all of the _____ .

    a. Philistines   b. Amalekites   c. Ammonites

1.010   David and Bathsheba were the parents of _____ .

    a. Adonijah   b. Solomon   c. Absalom

Match these items (each answer, 2 points).

1.011   _____ Uriah
1.012   _____ Michal
1.013   _____ Mephibosheth
1.014   _____ Joab
1.015   _____ Hiram
1.016   _____ Abishag
1.017   _____ Adonijah
1.018   _____ queen of Sheba
1.019   _____ Saul
1.020   _____ Araunah

a. David's first wife
b. sold a threshingfloor to David
c. Jonathan's father
d. tried to seize David's throne
e. cared for David in his old age
f. Jonathan's lame son
g. commander of David's troops
h. king of Tyre
i. Bathsheba's first husband
j. came to hear Solomon's wisdom

Complete these statements (each answer, 3 points).

1.021   God warns His people not to intermarry with _____ .

1.022   David's major sin was _____ .

1.023   Solomon's major sin was _____ .

1.024   Samuel went to _____ in search of a new king.

1.025   David was the son of _____ .

1.026   Solomon asked God for _____ .

1.027   Hiram provided Solomon with _____ to use in building the Temple.

1.028   Solomon recorded his wisdom in the form of _____ .

1.029   God appeared to Solomon in a dream at _____ .

1.030   Solomon was anointed king at a spring near _____ .

Answer *true* or *false* (each answer, 1 point).

1.031   _____ Each of the twelve sections of Solomon's kingdom were responsible for one year's provisions.

1.032   _____ Jerusalem housed the Ark of the Covenant.

1.033   _____ Solomon's wives encouraged him to worship God.

1.034   _____ David had to defend his throne.

1.035   _____ David was anointed king of Israel after Saul's death.

1.036   _____ Israel became a peaceful nation following Solomon's apostasy.

1.037   _____ Nathan encouraged Bathsheba to talk with David about Adonijah's intentions.

1.038   _____ Jerusalem was established as the city of David.

1.039   _____ David was rejected by the people of Saul's kingdom.

1.040   _____ David wrote Psalm 51 after his sin with Bathsheba.

Answer these questions (each answer, 5 points).

1.041   What were David's personality characteristics? _____
_____

1.042   How did Solomon identify the real mother of the dead child? _____
_____
_____

1.043   Whose deaths caused David to grieve? _____

1.044   What was Solomon's greatest contribution to future generations? _____
_____

80/100

Score _____
Adult check _____
Initial   Date

13

II. PSALMS AND PROVERBS

Psalms and Proverbs offer enjoyable reading and condense guidelines for Christian conduct. David's lyrics and Solomon's maxims help you with understanding your identity (Who am I?), dealing with crises (What do I do now?), and choosing a lifestyle (Where am I going? How will I get there?) In this section, you will involve yourself with the material of the Psalms and Proverbs through practical application to real life situations.

SECTION OBJECTIVES

Read this objective to learn what you should be able to do when you have completed this section.

6. Identify Scriptural examples of sanctification, comfort, God's omnipresence, His sovereignty, and guidance.

VOCABULARY

Study these words to enhance your learning success in this section.

brevity	incessant	omniscience
conspicuous	omnipotence	sanctify
frailty	omnipresence	sovereign

SANCTIFICATION

Christians are concerned about spiritual health, and cleanliness is a major factor. Although Christians are regenerated by God (their hearts turned from hatred toward love of God) our maturing in **sanctification** is defined by our consumption of God's Word.

> Wherewithal shall a young man
>   cleanse his way?
> By taking heed *thereto* according to
>   thy word.
> With my whole heart have I sought
>   thee:
> O let me not wander from thy
>   commandments.
> Thy word have I hid in mine heart,
>   that I might not sin against thee.
>   (Psalm 119:9-11)

The purpose of youth is to grow into adulthood, as we are constantly challenged from within and without in the process. On the way, we face many decisions about emotions, friendships, sexuality, politics, society, and religion. Through Scripture, God the Holy Spirit guides us toward correct decisions.

The success of our maturity into earthly adulthood depends upon two factors.

1. *Clearly define your goals.* Who would you like to be? What do you admire? What are you good at?
2. Act *based on your goals.* The people you associate with, places you go and things you do effect who you become. Associate with people and do things that directly support your goals.

Deceiving the Christian to subtly ignore the LORD (abandoning Scripture study, not attending services) is the most common method Satan uses to separate the believer from fellowship with God. Thus, the Psalmist asked for God's discipline to help him *keep* the commandments.

The only way you know who you are and where you are going is through the penetrating gaze of God's Word. Memorize Scripture. Hide God's Word in your heart as you meditate on His commandments, and He will guide your paths (Psalm 119:105).

Complete these activities.

2.1 Samuel, David, and Solomon were each concerned about sanctification. Read the following passages and, in your own words, write how each man responded to God's guidance and commands.

a. Samuel (1 Samuel 3:19): _____

_____

b. David (1 Samuel 18:14): _____

_____

14

c. Solomon (1 Kings 3:6-9): _____

_____

2.2   How does God's Word keep someone spiritually clean?

_____

_____

_____

_____

 Match these items. Match the beginning of each verse with its correct ending.

2.3   _____ With my whole heart have I sought thee:

                                  a. By taking heed *thereto* according to thy word.

2.4   _____ Wherewithal shall a young man cleanse his way?

                                  b. O let me not wander from thy commandments

                                  c. that I might not sin against thee.

2.5   _____ Thy word have I hid in mine heart,

Read Psalm 142.

COMFORT

Scholars believe Psalm 142 was written during David's escape from Saul to the cave near Adullam. He sought refuge in that cave and was later joined by his family and about four hundred men in distress (1 Samuel 22:1-2, 2 Samuel 23:13).

This Psalm was a confident supplication for God's protection and comfort during this frightening situation.

Psalm 142 is also a praise that proclaims the LORD is the Christian's refuge, Father, and Protector. God Himself is our portion in the land of the living. Without the inheritance of God's protective and divine care, the land of the living is a land of death. Even when your spirit is overwhelmed, be confident that then is the time God carries you through.

Although most do not fear for their physical life as David did, we all must face internal and external persecutors. We persecute ourselves and others we want to hurt or avoid.

David cried, "Bring my soul out of prison, that I may praise thy name..." (Psalm 142:7). He knew that only God could deliver him. David was not bargaining, but was offering God the promise of his praise. As Christians, we commit ourselves to praising and thanking God for *every* situation in which we find ourselves.

When you need comfort, the only place to find it is in communion with God. He nourishes and restores the souls of his children, according to His holy promise. Be assured that God hears and answers prayers according to His will, which brings Him glory. Especially in persecution, our goal is to glorify God.

Complete these statements.

2.6   Scholars believe that Psalm 142 was written during David's escape from

     _____ .

2.7   David sought physical refuge in a cave near _____ .

2.8   David sought spiritual refuge in _____ .

2.9   Psalm 142 is a confident _____ for God's protection and comfort.

2.10   David proclaimed that the Lord was his a. _____ and b. _____ in the land of the living.

2.11   Only _____ can deliver us from our enemies.

2.12   Christians strive to _____ God alone.

Complete these verses from Psalm 142.

2.13   "I cried unto the LORD with my a. _____ and with my voice did I make
        my b. _____ I poured out my c. _____ before him; I
        shewed before him my trouble" (v. 1-2).

2.14   "When my spirit was a. _____ within me, then thou knewest my
        b. _____ In the way wherein I walked have they privily laid a
        c. _____ for me" (v. 3).

2.15   "Attend unto my cry; for I am brought very low: a. _____ me from my
        b. _____ ; for they are stronger than I" (v. 6).

2.16   "Bring my soul out of a. _____ , that I may b. _____ thy
        name: the c. _____ shall compass me about; for thou shalt deal
        d. _____ with me" (v. 7).

Read Psalm 139.

GOD'S OMNIPRESENCE

One of the most assuring passages in Scripture is Psalm 139. David knew that God knew every detail of his life: his exact thoughts, speech, geographical location, and spiritual condition. He wrote in awe of God's **omnipresence**, **omniscience,** and **omnipotence**.

God knows all of your ways, and nothing is hidden from Him. He is constantly and intimately active in your life.

David, who well remembered being a fugitive, was delighted that there was nowhere to run from God. Heaven, hell, morning, or night are not inaccessible to Him. David proclaimed that God was ruler of all life from the moment of conception, praising Him for the miracle of life, for he was fearfully and wonderfully made.

God thinks about us **incessantly**. God's thoughts of you cannot be numbered. Do you know anyone else who thinks about you every second of the day? All Christians are His children and cares about them even when no one else seems to.

David was grieved that God has enemies. He considered God's enemies his own and committed their destiny to God. Does the sin of taking the LORD's name in vain grieve you as it did David?

In the closing verses of Psalm 139, David petitioned God to search the corners of his heart and reveal any concealed sin. Many times we sin out of ignorance of what we are doing and other sins are quickly disregarded. **Conspicuous** sins are quickly identified, but sins of attitude and thought easily escape without notice. God alone reveals to us the sin hidden deep inside.

Complete this activity.

2.17   Study carefully Psalm 139 and write a one-page paraphrase of it.

Score _____
Adult check _____
                Initial   Date

BIBLE

LIFEPAC TEST

80 / 100

Name _____

Date _____

Score _____

BIBLE 1209: LIFEPAC TEST

Answer *true* **or** *false* (each answer, 1 point).

1. _____ David was prudent in speech.
2. _____ Reading God's Word is vital to sanctification.
3. _____ Godly wisdom is required for effective problem solving.
4. _____ Araunah sold a threshingfloor to David.
5. _____ Being alert and active is a state of readiness.
6. _____ In the cave at Engedi, David cut off a piece of Saul's robe.
7. _____ The tongue is a destructive force.
8. _____ David's grief over the death of his loved ones caused him to write a proverb.
9. _____ Israel became a peaceful nation following Solomon's apostasy.
10. _____ The fulfillment of the Law and the prophets is the Old Testament.

Match these items (each answer, 2 points).

11. _____ Adonijah
12. _____ Solomon
13. _____ Mephibosheth
14. _____ Joab
15. _____ Elisabeth
16. _____ Asaph
17. _____ Saul
18. _____ queen of Sheba
19. _____ Agag
20. _____ Michal

a. commander of David's troops
b. king of the Amalekites
c. John the Baptist's mother
d. David's first wife
e. Jonathan's lame son
f. was jealous of David
g. tried to seize David's throne
h. brought gold and jewels to Solomon
i. David and Bathsheba's son
j. led music services for David and Solomon

Complete these statements (each answer, 3 points).

21. A prophetic saying of divine revelation is called an _____ .

22. David's major sin was _____ .

23. David had a covenant relationship with _____ .

24. David went to _____ for spiritual refuge.

25. God instructed His people not to intermarry with _____ .

26. David arranged the murder of Bathsheba's husband _____ .

27. Saul disobeyed _____ in not killing all of the Amalekites.

28. Spiritual _____ is a major factor in spiritual health.

29. God sent _____ to Bethlehem in search of a new king.

30. David was the son of _____ .

1

Choose the correct answer (each answer, 3 points).

31.   You must define and describe the _____ of a problem before solving it.
       a. extent   b. dynamics   c. definitions

32.   Psalm 139 speaks of God's _____ .
       a. omniscience   b. omnipresence   c. omnipotence

33.   To be disquieted means to be _____ .
       a. noisy   b. calm   c. disturbed

34.   In David's old age, he was cared for by _____ .
       a. Absalom   b. Abishag   c. Amalek

35.   The peaceful state of Israel came to an end following Solomon's _____ .
       a. adultery   b. adulation   c. apostasy

36.   Solomon asked God for _____ .
       a. wealth and riches   b. wisdom   c. love

37.   God appeared to Solomon in a dream at a spring near _____ .
       a. Gihon   b. Gibeon   c. Galilee

38.   Bathsheba was encouraged by _____ to talk with David concerning Adonijah.
       a. Nathan   b. Samuel   c. Solomon

39.   Solomon _____ the mother of the dead child.
       a. married   b. consoled   c. identified

40.   Bravery, mercy, humility, shrewdness, and prayer were qualities of _____ .
       a. Saul   b. Solomon   c. David

Answer these questions (each answer, 5 points).

41.   What was Solomon's greatest contribution to future generations?
       _____

42.   What is the ultimate solution to personal conflicts?
       _____

NOTES

Answer these questions. Use a dictionary if necessary.

2.18   What is meant by *omnipresence*? _____

_____

2.19   What is meant by *omnipotence*? _____

_____

2.20   What is meant by *omniscience*? _____

_____

 Read Psalm 39:1-8.

GOD'S SOVEREIGNTY

David understood the tongue's destructive force, and was afraid of his anger, lest he sin. In Psalm 39 David declared his commitment to control his anger and choose his words wisely, for prudent speech honors God.

David asked God to help him grasp life's **brevity**. He was keenly aware of death's certainty because he constantly witnessed the carnage of battle. He suffered the loss of his best friend, Jonathan, and Absalom, his beloved son. However, his own survival in the face of death allowed him to momentarily forget his own **frailty**.

Recognizing mortality is to realize that God is in control of the Universe. He alone has power over life and death. He numbers our days and decides by what means we will face death. Take heart, for your life is under the power of our loving, **sovereign** God. He plans and causes all things to work together for our good and His glory.

Each day counts. We are not promised tomorrow. What we fail to do today may go undone throughout eternity. God expects service from you in direct proportion to your capabilities. You have a contribution to make to God's kingdom regardless of your capabilities or your age.

Many people today have displaced hope. The focus of our life is a job promotion, increased salary, worldly recognition, friends, family, a better tomorrow, or improved technology. David knew that there is no hope apart from God, for he is the beginning and end of all things.

David's relationship with God was serious. He was responsible for God's reputation on earth. So are you. When you willfully transgress against God, you invite the condemnation of God's enemies, who await the chance to say, "I told you so." Always "let your light so shine before men, that they may see your good works, and glorify your Father which is in heaven" (Matthew 5:16).

 Complete this activity.

2.21   Use a dictionary or encyclopedia to find the meanings of these words from Psalm 39:1-8 and write the definition on the line.

a. musing (verse 3): _____

_____

b. handbreadth (verse 5): _____

_____

c. vanity (verse 5): _____

_____

d. disquieted (verse 6): _____

_____

Complete this activity.

2.22 Use a concordance to find other references to the destructive power of the tongue. List three of these Scripture references.

a. _____

b. _____

c. _____

 Read Proverbs 3:1-6.

GUIDANCE

Our own intellects have been darkened and our understanding shrouded by the Fall. Therefore, to understand any spiritual truths, we need divine guidance. God guides us every time we read His Word. His will for individual lives is clear and complete, especially in Christ's sacrifice. Keeping God's law perfectly is impossible among mankind, even among His redeemed. However, His laws are often practical and always in your best interest.

The primary teaching of the Law is that God is the center of all life "…In Him we live, and move, and have our being…" (Acts 17:28). The second teaching is our responsibility to reflect His character to the world, especially mercy and truth. Christ Himself did that perfectly, even unto the cross.

 Memorize Proverbs 3:5-6. Rewrite these verses from memory.

2.23 Proverbs 3:5 _____

_____

2.24 Proverbs 3:6 _____

_____

GOD'S GRACE IS OUR GUIDANCE.

Complete this activity.

2.25   Find and circle these words in the puzzle. Words may be horizontal, vertical, diagonal or backwards.

acknowledge	life	neck
truth	mercy	path
commandments	forsake	understanding
sight	bind	heart
direct	own	peace
favour		

```
C  E  N  N  E  C  K  N  O  V  R  S  O  W
R  O  J  D  I  R  E  C  T  A  O  Q  E  U
U  J  M  L  D  O  O  B  R  L  A  M  V  N
O  W  N  M  S  C  G  E  C  A  E  P  L  D
V  M  O  F  A  L  G  E  E  R  H  L  O  E
A  L  Y  O  A  N  D  N  I  B  E  T  V  R
F  M  C  R  S  P  D  O  I  T  A  H  M  S
A  P  R  S  N  E  M  M  M  E  R  G  T  T
C  Y  E  A  E  T  H  W  E  L  T  I  V  A
F  Y  M  K  A  T  O  N  Y  N  R  S  O  N
O  W  O  E  U  R  Z  Z  C  I  T  B  E  D
O  V  U  R  B  P  A  T  H  I  O  S  S  I
E  S  T  T  U  M  O  C  E  E  A  P  N  N
J  E  R  R  S  E  F  I  L  E  V  H  B  G
D  B  A  C  K  N  O  W  L  E  D  G  E  O
```

 Score _____
Adult check _____
                      Initial   Date

    Review the material in this section in preparation for the Self Test. This Self Test will check your mastery of this particular section. The items missed on this Self Test will indicate specific areas where restudy is needed for mastery.

Answer *true* **or** *false* (each answer, 1 point).

2.01 _____ Studying God's Word is part of Sanctification.

2.02 _____ Some scholars believe that Psalm 142 was written during David's escape from Saul.

2.03 _____ David proclaimed that Israel was his refuge and portion in the land of the living.

2.04 _____ David's major sin was idolatry.

2.05 _____ Psalm 139 speaks of God's omnipresence.

2.06 _____ Israel became a peaceful nation following Solomon's apostasy.

2.07 _____ God instructs His children not to intermarry with pagans.

2.08 _____ Sanctification has nothing to do with spiritual maturity.

2.09 _____ Abishag cared for Solomon in his old age.

2.10 _____ The Psalms David composed were supplications, thanksgivings, and oracles.

Match these items (each answer, 2 points).

2.011 _____ David's cave
a. growing in spiritual maturity; to make holy

2.012 _____ God is everywhere
b. reveals Man's inner thoughts and intents

2.013 _____ God is all powerful
c. omnipresence

2 014 _____ God is all knowing
d. enriched David's relationship to God

2.015 _____ musing
e. sold a threshingfloor to David

2.016 _____ Adonijah
f. tried to seize David's throne

2.017 _____ Araunah
g. omniscience

2.018 _____ prayer
h. thinking about something in a dreamy way

2.019 _____ God's Word
i. Adullam

2.020 _____ Sanctification
j. omnipotence

Complete these passages (each answer, 3 points).

2.021 "Wherewithal shall a young man _____ his way?" (Psalm 199:9)

2.022 "Thy word have I _____ in mine heart." (119:11a)

2.023 "With my whole heart I have _____ thee." (119:10a)

2.024 "With my voice unto the LORD did I make my _____ ." (142:1b)

2.025 "When my spirit was overwhelmed within me, then thou knewest my _____ ." (142:3a)

2.026 "Deliver me from my _____ ; for they are stronger than I." (142:6b)

2.027 "Bring my soul out of _____ , that I may praise thy name." (142:7a)

2.028 "The _____ shall compass me about." (142:7b)

2.029 "Trust in the LORD with all thine heart; and lean not unto thine own _____ ." (Proverbs 3:5)

2.030 "In all thy ways _____ him, and he shall direct thy paths." (3:6)

Choose the correct answer (each answer, 2 points).

2.031   David had all of these personal qualities *except* _____ .

         a. bravery   c. cowardice

         b. shrewdness   d. humility

2.032   The word disquieted has all these meanings *except* _____ .

         a. anxious   c. troubled

         b. restless   d. silent

2.033   The Psalms include each of these types *except* _____ .

         a. hymns   c. supplications

         b. fables   d. thanksgivings

2.034   The deaths of each of these people *except* _____ caused David much grief.

         a. Saul   c. Jonathan

         b. Solomon   d. Absalom

2.035   The Bible warns against the destructive force of _____ .

         a. the tongue   c. earthquakes

         b. the Flood   d. angels

Answer these questions (each answer, 5 points).

2.036   Where did David go for spiritual refuge? _____

2.037   What did David declare God to be for Him "in the land of the living?" _____

         _____

2.038   How did Saul disobey God? _____

         _____

         _____

2.039   What is a lament? _____

         _____

$\frac{72}{90}$

Score _____

Adult check _____

                              Initial   **Date**

III. BIBLICAL LITERATURE

Literary forms in the Bible are as diverse as the personalities of the writers that God used. Historical accounts, genealogies, laws, and dramas enliven the pages of Scripture along with both lyric and love poetry. While spiritual truths are written through prose, commandments, and parables.

SECTION OBJECTIVES

Review these objectives. When you have completed this section, you should be able to:

8. Describe the importance of wisdom in problem solving,

9. Name three types of Davidic Psalms,

10. Describe the Biblical literary styles, and

11. Identify New Testament examples of prefiguration in the Old Testament.

VOCABULARY

Study these words to enhance your learning success in this section.

affinity	narrative	prefiguration
liturgy	oracle	

LITERARY STYLE

The Old Testament is divided into books of Law, History, Poetry, and Prophecy.

The Law and Historical books are written in dramatic and detailed **narrative** prose. The Law books (Pentateuch) are Genesis, Exodus, Leviticus, Numbers, and Deuteronomy. The Historical books are Joshua, Judges, Ruth, 1 and 2 Samuel, 1 and 2 Kings, 1 and 2 Chronicles, Ezra, Nehemiah, and Esther.

The Poetical books are books of wisdom and devotion written in poetic and proverbial forms. They are Job, Psalms, Proverbs, Ecclesiastes, and The Song of Solomon.

The Prophecy books are Isaiah, Jeremiah, Lamentations, Ezekiel, Daniel, Hosea, Joel, Amos, Obadiah, Jonah, Micah, Nahum, Habakkuk, Zephaniah, Haggai, Zechariah, and Malachi. These use three basic literary styles. One style is that of **oracles**, prophetic sayings with a teaching whose originator is either God or the prophet speaking in his name. The other two styles are narratives, spoken in either the first or third person.

Psalms. The psalms are prophetic and often address the king. Three general classifications are hymns, supplications, and thanksgivings. A few do not fit any of these groups, and variations occur within each one. Royal Psalms generally describe, praise, and anticipate the king; yet the messages contain the feelings and prayers of mankind as a whole.

1. *Hymns.* Usually written above hymns is the word *mizmor*, meaning musical accompaniment, the word *song* or *psalm*. They are hymns of praise, of the "Songs of Zion" and Psalms of God's Kingship.

2. *Supplications.* The Psalms of supplication are collective or individual exclamations of lament and suffering. They describe misfortune and represent the author's effort to convince God of the immediate need of their cause. God is true to His former mercies, and often proves Himself king.

3. *Thanksgivings.* Many Psalms close with thanksgiving, but it is the main theme for others. Man has much to be grateful for materially and spiritually.

Because the Psalms were composed as musical prayers, they were sung or recited by the individuals within a community. These worship poems, generally public in nature and direction, were written for **liturgy** in the Temple or private meditation.

Israel's hymnal, the Psalter, contained a collection of 150 Psalms. Although David is traditionally asserted to be the author of the book of Psalms, he did share authorship with others. The Hebrew text attributes 73 Psalms to David, and the Septuagint assigns 82.

However, scholars indicate that inscriptions on the Psalms sometimes point to **affinity** rather than authorship.

Asaph's family headed the music services during David and Solomon's collective reigns. Asaph wrote twelve and Korah wrote eleven Psalms. The Temple singers (cantors) were the "sons of Asaph," and the "sons of Korah." These cantor families have specific collections of Psalms with authorship attributed to Asaph or Korah. Heman, Ethan (or Jeduthun), Moses and Solomon are each credited with having written at least one. About one-third of the Psalms have no specified authorship.

New Testament. Jesus is presented in the New Testament as the fulfillment of the Law and the prophets. Reflections of Old Testament style are seen throughout the New Testament in genealogies, narrative, parables, psalms, proverbs, and prophecy. The Old Testament is the description and anticipation of who Jesus was to be, while the New Testament is the expression and fulfillment of who Jesus is.

Complete these activities.

3.1   Name the four divisions of the Old Testament.

a. _____

b. _____

c. _____

d. _____

3.2   List the five Poetry books of the Old Testament.

a. _____

b. _____

c. _____

d. _____

e. _____

3.3   Name the three general classifications of Psalms.

a. _____

b. _____

c. _____

Match these items.

3.4   _____ mizmor

3.5   _____ oracle

3.6   _____ royal Psalm

3.7   _____ narrative

3.8   _____ Psalm of supplication

3.9   _____ the Psalter

3.10   _____ Asaph

3.11   _____ Ethan

3.12   _____ Jesus

3.13   _____ Old Testament

3.14   _____ David

a. also known as Jeduthun

b. led music services for David and Solomon

c. fulfillment of the Law and prophets

d. divine revelation

e. denotes musical accompaniment

f. Israel's hymnbook

g. exclamation of lament and suffering

h. spoken in the first or third person

i. generally praise, anticipating the king

j. wrote most of the Psalms

k. describes and anticipates who Jesus was to be

PREFIGURATION

The two time segments significant to pre-incarnate history are the periods from Abraham to David and from David to Jesus. David was a **prefiguration** of Jesus, the King and Shepherd of God's children. Many of David's Psalms refer directly to events in Christ's life.

David and Jesus. Similarities in the lives of David and Jesus are evident from birth to death. Samuel the prophet experienced the honor of anointing David as king. John the Baptist, born to Elisabeth in her old age, was the prophet who baptized Jesus at the beginning of public ministry. In David's time, Israel wanted a king to conquer the pagan Philistines. In the time of Jesus, Israel was reaching toward a king to overthrow the bondage of Roman rule. David led God's people to safety in Israel. Jesus brought salvation to man and established believers under the authority of the kingdom of God.

As a shepherd, David nurtured and cared for his sheep and attended to his spiritual development on the hills of Bethlehem. Jesus is also called a Shepherd because He nurtures and cares for His followers. In the village of Nazareth, Jesus grew in stature before the LORD.

The young David astounded the soldiers and King Saul by his precise, articulate, and convincing words that he would fight and kill the Philistine giant. Goliath had insulted God, and David was confident that, "in the name of the LORD of hosts," he could conquer him. The young Jesus astounded the scholars in the Temple with his questions and answers which showed a clear insight. He announced His mission by saying that He must be about His Father's business. Christ's task was to conquer sin. David was enraged that Goliath was blaspheming God, and Jesus was angered by those who established a market place in the Temple of God.

David was hunted by Saul, who was influenced by an evil spirit. Saul feared David's public appeal would lead the people to crown David king. Saul's fear of losing the throne inspired his jealousy. Jesus was sought by the Pharisees and rulers of Israel because they were afraid that the people would proclaim Him king. The Pharisees, who abused the Law to serve their own vanities, were afraid that Jesus was taking over their authority.

David was exiled to the enemy territory in Ziklag, and Jesus had no place to lay His head. David lamented Saul and Jonathan's death, while

David's Shepherding was a Prefiguration of Christ's

Jesus wept over Lazarus and Jerusalem.

David was king over Judah and all Israel. He danced before the LORD as the Ark was brought to Jerusalem. Jesus' Triumphal Entry was one of kingly honor and praise. He is now King over the spiritual Kingdom of His elect.

David's son Absalom betrayed him and sought to usurp the throne. Jesus was betrayed by His friend and disciple, Judas.

David reigned in Jerusalem for thirty-three years. Jesus lived about thirty-three years and is the eternal King of Kings.

The following chart indicates passages in Psalms and Proverbs that are topically echoed in the New Testament. Study the passages and observe the harmony and unity between Old and New Testaments.

PSALM OR PROVERB	SUBJECT	NEW TESTAMENT
Psalm 130:8	REDEEM ISRAEL FROM SIN	Matthew 1:21
Psalm 72:10	WORSHIP OF MAGI	Matthew 2:11
Psalm 91:11-12	TEMPTATION IN WILDERNESS	Luke 4:10
Psalm 37:11 Proverbs 2:21	SERMON ON THE MOUNT	Luke 6:20-23
Psalm 139:2-3	ALMSGIVING	Matthew 6:4
Psalm 62:10	GOD AND MONEY	Matthew 6:24
Psalm 145:15	TRUST IN GOD'S CARE	Matthew 6:25-26
Proverbs 17:4	NEW STANDARD HIGHER	Matthew 5:23-24
Proverbs 20:6	PRAYER IN SECRET	Matthew 6:5
Proverbs 30:8-9 Proverbs 24:29 Proverbs 21:13	LORD'S PRAYER	Luke 11:2-4
Proverbs 20:6	FAST IN SECRET	Matthew 6:16
Psalm 62:10	TRUE TREASURE	Matthew 6:20
Proverbs 20:27	EYE IS THE LAMP OF BODY	Luke 11:34-35
Psalm 36:2	DO NOT JUDGE	Luke 6:37-42
Proverbs 23:9	PROFANING SACRED THINGS	Matthew 7:6
Proverbs 8:17	EFFECTIVE PRAYER	Matthew 7:8 Mark 11:24
Proverbs 3:27	GOLDEN RULE	Matthew 7:12

PSALM OR PROVERB	SUBJECT	NEW TESTAMENT
Psalm 5:5; 6:8	TRUE DISCIPLE	Luke 6:46-47
Psalm 33:9; 107:20	CURE OF SERVANT	John 4:46-53
Psalm 88:3; 11-19	HARDSHIPS OF APOSTOLIC CALLING	Luke 9:57-60
Psalm 107:29; 65:7	CALMING STORM	Matthew 8:27
Proverbs 11:25	CUP OF WATER	Mark 9:41
Proverbs 10:14	WORDS BETRAY HEART	Matthew 12:35 ·
Proverbs 2:4	TREASURE	Matthew 13:44
Psalm 78:36	TRADITION OF PHARISEE	Mark 7:6
Psalm 62:12	JUDGEMENT OF GOD	Matthew 16:27
Psalm 131:2	WHO IS GREATEST	Matthew 18:3
Psalm 118:26	ENTERS JERUSALEM	John 12:12-16
Psalm 110:1	CHRIST, SON, AND LORD OF DAVID	Matthew 22:41-46
Psalm 75:6	TRIBULATION OF JERUSALEM	Luke 17:23-24
Proverbs 14:35	CONSCIENTIOUS STEWARD	Matthew 24:45 Luke 12:41-48
Proverbs 19:17	LAST JUDGEMENT	Matthew 25:40
Psalm 55:13-14	TREACHERY OF JUDAS	Matthew chapter 26
Proverbs 27:6	ARREST OF JESUS	Matthew 26:49-50
Psalm 35:11	JESUS BEFORE SANHEDRIN	Matthew 26:59
Psalm 22:7-8	CRUCIFIED CHRIST MOCKED	Matthew 27:39-43
Psalm 22:1	DEATH OF JESUS	Matthew 27:46
Psalm 125:2	MISSION TO WORLD	Matthew 28:20

Complete these statements.

3.15   Hannah is to a. _____ as Elisabeth is to b. _____ .

3.16   In David's time, Israel needed a king to conquer the pagan _____ .

3.17   In Jesus' day, Israel wanted a king to overthrow _____ rule.

3.18   David and Jesus both displayed nurturing and caring qualities similar to the responsibilities of a _____ .

3.19   Saul was astounded by _____ convincing words.

3.20   David was hunted by _____ .

3.21   Jesus was sought by the a. _____ and b. _____ of Israel.

3.22   David was exiled to the territory of a. _____ while Jesus had no place to b. _____ .

3.23   David was betrayed by a. _____ and Jesus was betrayed by b. _____ .

Answer this question.

3.24   What is meant by *prefiguration*? _____

_____

_____

Psalms and Proverbs. The fulfillment of the prefigurations in Psalms and Proverbs came through the New Testament. The mission of the coming Messiah as recorded in Matthew 1:21 is almost a quote from Psalm 130:8: "And he shall redeem Israel from all his iniquities."

The Beatitudes in Matthew 5, clearly reflect the Psalms. "But the meek shall inherit the earth…" (Psalm 37:11). "They that sow in tears shall reap in joy." (Psalm 126:5).

Psalm 34:14 admonished, "Depart from evil, and do good; seek peace, and pursue it." Proverbs 12:20 states, "Deceit *is* in the heart of them that imagine evil: but to the counsellors of peace *is* joy." Jesus said, "Blessed *are* the peacemakers: for they shall be called the children of God" (Matthew 5:9).

Jesus' word cured the nobleman's son who lay dying in a neighboring city (John 4:46-54). "He sent his word, and healed them, and delivered them from their destructions" (Psalm 107:20).

The LORD Jesus, delivers the redeemed from the wrath of God's holiness. "He maketh the storm a calm, so that the waves thereof are still" (Psalm 107:29). "But the men marveled, saying, "What manner of man is this, that even the winds and the sea obey him" (Matthew 8:27)!

Psalm 78:36 dramatizes Jesus' relationship with the Pharisees, "Nevertheless they did flatter him with their mouth, and they lied unto him with their tongues." Jesus uncovered their disgusting insincerity, "…This people honoureth me with their lips, but their heart is far from me" (Mark 7:6).

Foretelling His future glory and the Judgement, Jesus exclaimed, "For the Son of man shall come in the glory of his Father with his angels; and then he shall reward every man according to his works" (Matthew 16:27). Psalm 62:12 echoes, "Also unto thee, O LORD, *belongeth* mercy: for thou renderest to every man according to his work."

At Christ's Triumphal Entry into Jerusalem, the crowds of people shouted, "Blessed *be* he that cometh in the name of the LORD…" (Psalm 118:26). Both Jesus and David were triumphant kings.

Psalm 22:6-8 predicts Christ's ridicule. "But I *am* a worm, and no man; a reproach of men, and despised of the people. All they that see me laugh me to scorn: they shoot out the lip, they shake the head, *saying*, He trusted on the LORD *that* he would deliver him: let him deliver him, seeing he delighted in him." Mark 15:29-30 is the fulfillment of the Psalmist's prediction, "And they that passed by railed on him, wagging their heads, and saying, Ah, thou that destroyeth the temple, and buildest *it* in three days, Save thyself, and come down from the cross."

Match these items. Match the New Testament incident with the Old Testament prefiguration.

3.25 _____ the Messiah saves His people

3.26 _____ Jesus blesses the peacemakers

3.27 _____ Jesus cures the nobleman's son

3.28 _____ the winds and the sea obeyed Jesus

3.29 _____ Jesus' relationship with the Pharisees

3.30 _____ The Judgement

3.31 _____ The Triumphal Entry

3.32 _____ The Crucifixion

a. "Blessed is he that cometh in the name of the LORD."

b. "Nevertheless they did flatter me with their mouth, and they lied unto me with their tongues."

c. "He maketh the storm a calm, so that the waves thereof are still."

d. "He sent his word, and healed them, and delivered them from their destructions."

e. "Also unto thee, O LORD, belongeth mercy: for thou renderest every man according to his work."

f. "But I am a worm, and no man; a reproach of man, and despised of the people."

g. "Deceit is in the heart of them that imagine evil: but to the counselors of peace is joy."

h. "And he shall redeem Israel from all his iniquities."

 Read Proverbs 8:1-6.

PROBLEM SOLVING

We are constantly faced with conflicts that require decisions. Problem solving is not easy, but it is simplified by the guidance of the Scriptures. Problems are but opportunities to put God's Word into practice. Welcome personal conflicts and problems with the confidence that God uses them to mold, strengthen, and test your character.

Godly wisdom. Proverbs 6:9 questions, "How long wilt thou sleep, O sluggard? when wilt thou arise out of thy sleep?" Jesus said, "Blessed *are* those servants, whom the lord when he cometh shall find watching..." (Luke 12:37). Therefore, be alert and active.

Godly wisdom is required for effective problem solving. Wisdom speaks to all generations, but few listen. Acquire wisdom by humbly asking God for it. He will give it to you. "If any of you lack wisdom, let him ask of God, that giveth to all *men* liberally, and upbraideth not; and it shall be given him" (James 1:5).

Jesus described those who in their pride cannot hear His words: "...By hearing ye shall hear, and shall not understand; and seeing ye shall see, and shall not perceive" (Matthew 13:14).

HONESTLY EXAMINE YOURSELF

With each challenge, David composed his trust and began to thank God. David prayed fervently.

Evaluating problems. When you have recognized that a problem exists, you then begin defining and describing it's extent. Three practical methods of problem evaluation are (1) prayer with honest self-examination, (2) reading Scriptures and classic Christian literature, and (3) seeking wise counsel.

Like David, turn to God with your troubles and trust Him for strength. Ask God to deliver you, praising and thanking God for His past goodness.

Remember that the beginning of all problems is personal sin. For a clear measure of sin itself, look to the Law. The Law is a better gauge than are the lives of biblical characters (save Christ) for they were all uneven, human examples.

Count the cost. Consider the number of people involved and the possible effects of each option you have to choose from.

David's Psalms ask: Who is trustworthy? Is anyone on my side? Where is God? They express longing for worship and spiritual refuge. Solomon's Proverbs solve problems of authority, family relationships, and money.

Listen to the wisdom of others. Although young generations contend that parents are harsh in their judgment of contemporary lifestyles, God declares that wisdom is the same from generation to generation: "Hear, ye children, the instruction of a father, and attend to know understanding. For I give you good doctrine, forsake ye not my law. For I was my father's son, tender and only *beloved* in the

LISTEN TO THE WISDOM OF OTHERS

sight of my mother. He taught me also, and said unto me, Let thine heart retain my words: keep my commandments, and live" (Proverbs 4:1-4).

Taking Action. After evaluation, you must take action. David recognized his guilt. He admitted his sin and repented through prayer and fasting, embracing the consequences of his foolishness.

No one but Christ has ever had to deal with the sins of the world. Before His agony, he resigned to the Father's will. "Father if thou be willing, remove this cup from me: nevertheless, not my will, but thine, be done" (Luke 22:42). His life was devoted to the Father's glory, not His own, which is the ultimate solution to personal conflict.

Complete these statements.

3.33   Both Christ and Proverbs admonish men to be _____ .

3.34   Problems present _____ to put into practice what God's Word teaches.

3.35   A requirement for effective problem solving is godly _____ .

3.36   David _____ fervently.

3.37   _____ speaks to all generations.

3.38   Count the _____ of each option.

3.39   The beginning of all problems is personal _____ .

3.40   You must define and describe the _____ of the problem.

3.41   After evaluation, you must take _____ .

Answer these questions.

3.42   What are three practical methods of problem evaluation?

a. _____

b. _____

_____

c. _____

3.43   What is the ultimate solution to personal conflicts?

_____

Score _____

Adult check _____

            Initial   **Date**

Before you take this last Self Test, you may want to do one or more of these self checks.

1. _____ Read the objectives. Determine if you can do them.

2. _____ Restudy the material related to any objectives that you cannot do.

3. _____ Use the SQ3R study procedure to review the material:
   a. **S**can the sections.
   b. **Q**uestion yourself again (review the questions you wrote initially).
   c. **R**ead to answer your questions.
   d. **R**ecite the answers to yourself.
   e. **R**eview areas you didn't understand.

4. _____ Review all activities and Self Tests, writing a correct answer for each wrong answer.

Choose the correct answer (each answer, 2 points).

3.01   The family of _____ led music services during the reigns of David and Solomon.

    a. Ethan   b. Asaph   c. Aesop

3.02   A prophetic saying with a teaching is called an _____ .

    a. oracle   b. oration   c. aria

3.03   _____ is the fulfillment of the Law and the prophets.

    a. The New Testament   b. The Old Testament   c. Jesus

3.04   Hannah is to Samuel as Elisabeth is to _____ .

    a. Jesus   b. John the Baptist   c. David

3.05   God instructs His people not to intermarry with _____ .

    a. Jews   b. Israelites   c. pagans

3.06   Being alert and active is a state of _____ .

    a. readiness   b. purity   c. awareness

3.07   Yo must define and describe the _____ of a problem.

    a. extent   b. definition   c. dynamics

3.08   Psalm 139 speaks mainly of God's _____ .

    a. omniscience   b. omnipotence   c. omnipresence

3.09   David and _____ had a covenant relationship.

    a. Saul   b. Samuel   c. Jonathan

3.010   David was _____ in speech.

    a. pious   b. prudent   c. proud

Answer *true* **or** *false* (each answer, 1 point).

3.011   _____ David was the first husband of Bathsheba.

3.012   _____ Jerusalem was established as the city of David.

3.013   _____ Adonijah, Solomon's half-brother, wanted to become king of Israel.

3.014   _____ Israel's peaceful state came to an end following Solomon's apostasy.

3.015   _____ Solomon prayed for wealth and riches.

3.016   _____ God instructs His people not to worship false gods.

3.017   _____ David proclaimed that God was his refuge and portion in the land of the living.

3.018   _____ Godly wisdom is a requirement for effective problem solving.

3.019   _____ Wisdom speaks to all generations, but few listen.

3.020   _____ Problem solving begins by talking to others.

Complete these statements (each answer, 3 points).

3.021   The beginning of all problems is personal _____ .

3.022   Problems present _____ to put into practice what God's Word teaches.

3.023   The scholars in the Temple were astounded by the questions and understanding of

    _____ .

3.024   David and Jesus were both _____ of their people.

3.025   David was exiled to the territory of _____ .

3.026   Jesus was betrayed by _____ .

3.027   Solomon referred to all worldly pleasure as _____ .

3.028   Some scholars believe that Psalm 142 was written while David was _____
          from Saul.

3.029   Only _____ can deliver us from our enemies.

Match these items (each answer, 2 points).

3.030   _____ omnipotence   a. king of the Amalekites
3.031   _____ Araunah   b. denotes musical accompaniment
3.032   _____ lament   c. poem of grief and sorrow
3.033   _____ idolatry   d. all powerful
3.034   _____ royal Psalm   e. sold a threshingfloor to David
3.035   _____ Adullam   f. Pentateuch
3.036   _____ Agag   g. cave where David hid
3.037   _____ the Law books   h. anticipates the king
3.038   _____ mizmor   i. Solomon's sin

Answer these questions (each answer, 5 points).

3.039   What is meant by *prefiguration*? _____
          _____

3.040   What are two practical methods of problem evaluation?
          a. _____
          _____
          b. _____
          _____

3 041   What is the ultimate solution to personal conflicts? _____
          _____

3.042   What are the divisions of the Old Testament? _____
          _____

80 / 100

Score
Adult check _____
          Initial   Date

Before you take the LIFEPAC Test, you may want to do one or more of these self checks.

1. ____ Read the objectives. Determine if you can do them.
2. ____ Restudy the material related to any objectives that you cannot do.
3. ____ Use the SQ3R study procedure to review the material.
4. ____ Review all activities and Self Tests, and LIFEPAC Glossary.
5. ____ Restudy areas of weakness indicated by the last Self Test.

GLOSSARY

affinity. A condition of close relationship or resemblance.

apostasy. A complete forsaking of one's faith.

brevity. Shortness in writing or speech.

conspicuous. Easily seen.

covenant. A binding or solemn agreement between two parties.

ephah. An ancient Hebrew dry measure that is equivalent to approximately twenty-one quarts.

expertise. Expert opinion or knowledge.

frailty. Moral weakness; liability to yield to temptation.

incessant. Never stopping.

liturgy. A form of public worship.

narrative. A story or account of real events or experiences.

Omnipotence. All powerful.

Omnipresence. Present everywhere at the same time.

Omniscience. Having knowledge of everything.

Oracle. Divine revelation.

pestilence. Any disease that spreads rapidly causing many deaths.

prefiguration. An antecedent figure or type; a foreshadow; a prototype.

prudent. Sensible; wise; cautious.

remorse. Deep, painful regret for having done wrong.

sanctify. To make holy; to make spiritually mature.

sovereign. Supreme power and authority.

supplication. A humble and earnest request or prayer.

threshingfloor. A hard floor upon which oxen grind grain.

NOTES